Words of Life

Jesus and the Promise of the Ten Commandments Today

Adam Hamilton

Bestselling Author of *Making Sense of the Bible*

LEADER GUIDE

Abingdon Press | Nashville

Words of Life
Jesus and the Promise of
the Ten Commandments Today
Leader Guide

978-1-7910-1324-0

20 21 22 23 24 25 26 27 28 29—10 9 8 7 6 5 4 3 2 1
MANUFACTURED IN THE UNITED STATES OF AMERICA

CONTENTS

To the Leader 5

1. At the Center of It All 11

2. The Idols We Keep 17

3. "I Swear to God!" 22

4. Rediscovering the Joy of Sabbath 27

5. A Question of Honor 33

6. The Tragedy of Violence, the Beauty of Mercy 38

7. Faithfulness in an Age of Porn 44

8. We're All Thieves. Yes, Even You. 49

9. Sticks, Stones, and the Power of Words 54

10. Keeping Up with the Joneses 59

TO THE LEADER

Welcome! Thank you for serving as the facilitator for this study of *Words of Life: Jesus and the Promise of the Ten Commandments Today* by Adam Hamilton. In this study, we will look at each of the Ten Commandments God gave the ancient Israelites, the principles behind them, the way Jesus spoke to them and lived them, and, ultimately, how they speak to our lives today.

We'll learn that these commands are not just ancient codes of conduct, but are guardrails and guideposts that God has provided to help us live an abundant life and know God's heart in a deeper way.

This study makes use of the following components:

- the book *Words of Life: Jesus and the Promise of the Ten Commandments Today* by Adam Hamilton;
- this Leader Guide; and
- a DVD with video segments for each of the ten chapters in the book.

The study is broken into ten sessions, one for each commandment; however, depending on the time frame appropriate for your group, you can also choose to combine sessions to create a five- or six-week study:

- For a **ten-week study** with your group, study one commandment each week.
- For a **five-week study**, study two commandments each week.
- For a **six-week study**, we recommend the following:
  - ◊ Week 1: Commandments 1 and 2
  - ◊ Week 2: Commandments 3 and 4
  - ◊ Week 3: Commandment 5

◊   Week 4: Commandments 6 and 7
◊   Week 5: Commandments 8 and 9
◊   Week 6: Commandment 10

Regardless of which format you choose, it will be helpful if participants obtain a copy of the book *Words of Life* in advance and read the first chapter before the first session. Each participant will need a Bible. A notebook or journal is also recommended for taking notes, recording insights, and noting questions during the study.

Session Format

Every group is different. These session plans have been designed to give you flexibility and choices, so a variety of activities and discussion questions are included.

You will want to read the section titled "Before the Session" in this Leader Guide several days in advance of your meeting time so you can prepare as needed. As you plan each session, keep the session goals in mind and select the activities and discussion questions that will be most meaningful for your group. You will likely not have time to cover every discussion point.

The questions in "Getting Started" are designed to help participants begin to focus on the main topics for the session. Watch your time here so you will have time for the in-depth study later in the session.

This is a video-based study, so each session should begin with viewing the video followed by discussion of the video, book, and scripture passage.

Note: If your group chooses a five- or six-week study and will be combining commandments, plan to watch the second video after wrapping up discussion of the first video. Select ahead of time which discussion questions best fit the personality of the group, and decide how much time you want to allow for each part of the session plan.

The section "Wrapping Up" is designed to give partici-pants the opportunity to reflect on and process the various themes and topics covered in the session, as these relate to their own growing relationship with Jesus Christ.

Each session plan follows this outline:

Planning the Session
• Session Goals
• Biblical Foundation
• Before the Session

Getting Started
• Opening Activities
• Opening Prayer

Learning Together
• Video Viewing and Discussion
• Study and Discussion

Wrapping Up
• Closing Discussion
• Closing Prayer

Preparing for the Session

As you prepare for each session, be sure to do the following:

• Pray for the leading of the Holy Spirit as you prepare for the study. Pray for discernment for yourself and for each member of the study group.
• Before each session, familiarize yourself with the content. Read the book chapter again and watch the video segment.
• Choose the elements you will use during the group session, including the specific discussion questions you plan to cover. Be prepared, however, to adjust the

session as group members interact and as questions arise. Prepare carefully, but allow space for the Holy Spirit to move in and through the material, the group members, and you as facilitator.

- Secure in advance a TV and DVD player or a computer with projection.
- Prepare the space so that it will enhance the learning process. Ideally, group members should be seated around a table or in a circle so that all can see one another.
- Bring a supply of Bibles for those who forget to bring their own. Having a variety of translations is helpful. Also provide nametags and, if possible, have a few extra copies of *Words of Life* available.
- We suggest you have a whiteboard and markers, a chalkboard and chalk, or an easel with paper and markers available for your sessions as well, so that you can write down and then display throughout the session the commandment(s) you are studying. You may also need a writing surface for other activities and discussion.

Shaping the Learning Environment

Here are some helpful tips to keep in mind as you lead each session:

- Begin and end on time. If a session is running longer than expected, get consensus from the group before continuing beyond the agreed-upon ending time.
- Create a climate of openness, encouraging group members to participate as they feel comfortable. Remember that some people will jump right in with answers and comments, while others will need time to process what is being discussed.

8

- If you notice that some group members don't enter the conversation, ask them if they have thoughts to share. Give everyone a chance to talk, but keep the conversation moving. Try to prevent a few individuals from doing all the talking.
- Communicate the importance of group discussions and group exercises.
- If no one answers at first during discussions, don't be afraid of pauses. Count silently to ten; then say something such as, "Would anyone like to go first?" If no one responds, venture an answer yourself and ask for comments.
- Model openness as you share with the group. Group members will follow your example. If you limit your sharing to a surface level, others will follow suit.
- Encourage multiple answers or responses before moving on.
- Ask "Why?" or "Why do you believe that?" or "Can you say more about that?" to help continue a discussion and give it greater depth.
- Affirm others' responses with comments such as "Great" or "Thanks" or "Good insight"—especially if this is the first time someone has spoken during the group session.
- Monitor your own contributions. If you find yourself doing most of the talking, back off so that you don't train the group to listen rather than speak up.
- Remember that you don't have all the answers. Your job is to keep the discussion going and encourage participation.
- Involve group members in various aspects of the group session, such as playing the DVD, saying prayers, or reading the scripture.
- Note that the session plans sometimes call for breaking into smaller groups. This gives everyone a chance to speak and participate fully. Mix up the

teams; don't let the same people pair up on every activity.

- Because many activities call for personal sharing, confidentiality is essential. Group members should never pass along stories that have been shared in the group. Remind the group members at each session: confidentiality is crucial to the success of this study.

We pray that this will be a rich study for you and that you will find that these commandments serve as an anchor in today's ever-shifting moral seas. We also pray that you see the heart of Jesus revealed through each commandment as he calls us deeper into relationship.

ONE

AT THE CENTER OF IT ALL

Planning the Session

Session Goals

Through conversation, activities, and reflection, participants will:

- learn about the context in which God delivered the commandments to the Israelites;
- consider how the first commandment applies to their lives; and
- discover how Jesus interprets the first commandment in the New Testament.

Biblical Foundation

Exodus 20:1-3; Exodus 3:1-15; Ephesians 2:8-10a; Matthew 22:37-38

Before the Session

- Set up a table in the room with nametags, markers, Bibles, extra copies of *Words of Life*, paper, and pencils or pens.
- Prepare your DVD player or computer to play this week's video segment.
- If possible, have a whiteboard or chart paper and markers or a chalkboard and chalk available for use during the session. Write this session's commandment so that it is visible for all participants:

11

*I am the LORD your God who brought you out
of Egypt, out of the house of slavery. You must
have no other gods before me.*

(Exodus 20:2-3)

Getting Started

Opening Activities

Greet participants as they arrive. Invite them to make a nametag and, if available, pick up either a Bible or a copy of *Words of Life*, or both if they did not bring either.

Introductions

Introduce yourself. You may want to share why you are excited about teaching this Bible study about the Ten Commandments.

If you sense that the participants in your group do not know one another well, allow time for them to introduce themselves and share something about their relationship with the church—for example, the name of a Sunday school class or small group to which they belong, a mission project they support, which worship service they attend, or if they are a visitor. Extend a special welcome to anyone who does not regularly attend your church and invite her or him to worship at your church if the person does not have a church home.

Housekeeping

- Share any necessary information about your meeting space and parking.
- Let participants know you will be faithful to the scheduled meeting time, and encourage everyone to arrive on time.
- Encourage participants to read the upcoming chapter(s) before the next session.

- You may want to invite participants to have a note-book, journal, or electronic tablet for use during this study. Explain that these can be used to record questions and insights they have as they read each chapter and to take notes during each session.
- Ask participants to respect a policy of confidentiality within the group.

Leading into the Study

Ask participants to share:

- What has been your experience with the Ten Commandments? Were you taught them in church or school or at home?
- Have you, like the author's wife, wondered if the commandments are still relevant to believers today?
- Why are you interested in doing this study?

Opening Prayer

Holy God, we thank you for the opportunity to gather today and study your word to us. Open our ears and our hearts so that we can learn more about you and your desire for us as we learn more about leading lives that honor you; in Jesus's name. Amen.

Learning Together

Video Viewing and Discussion

Play the DVD session (each is approximately 10 minutes long), then invite the group to discuss:

- What thoughts or feelings arise as you watched the sun rise over Mount Sinai? After watching this, what do you imagine about Moses's time on the mountain with God?

13

- How do the shots of Mount Sinai help you imagine the setting the ancient Israelites were living in? What can you infer about their lives?
- What did you learn from the author's conversation with Rabbi Nemitoff?
- Adam Hamilton asks us to consider the ways in which we are tempted to edge God out, or to put something else in God's place in our lives. How might you answer that question?

Study and Discussion

In Exodus 3, we read about God calling Moses to lead God's people, the Israelites, out of slavery and to become a new nation.

- Read aloud, or invite a volunteer to read aloud, Exodus 3:1-15.
- What is God's stated desire for God's people in verses 7-8? (*to rescue them out of slavery and to take them to a new land of promise and plenty*)
- Hamilton points out that the Israelites would have known the names of hundreds, perhaps thousands, of the gods of Egypt. Moses says to God, "If I now come to the Israelites and say to them, 'The God of your ancestors has sent me to you,' they are going to ask me, 'What's this God's name?' What am I supposed to say to them?" (v. 13). In verses 14-15, in what two important ways does God define himself to the Israelites? (*"I Am," the creator of all things / the God of the Israelites' ancestors, therefore the Lord is their God— the Lord has chosen them.*)
- How do you imagine the Israelites—who were, at that point, persecuted and enslaved—responded to this idea that they were favored and chosen, that there was a God who wanted them to be free and prosper?

14

- Throughout Scripture, we see that God often chooses the powerless and the poor. God does this because compassion, mercy, justice, and love define God's nature. How does this relate to what Paul says in the New Testament, in Ephesians 2:8-10a?

As the Book of Exodus continues, we see the Lord use Moses to lead the Israelites out of slavery, and into the desert, where they await further instruction. Moses goes up Mount Sinai to meet with God and comes down with words from the Lord on two tablets (Exodus 32:15-16). Hamilton points out that most scholars believe the first tablet contained the first four commandments, which are about living in right relationship with God, and that the next six commandments, involving how we relate to our neighbor, were on the second tablet. These commandments were intended to set the guidelines for the new nation of Israel.

Read aloud, or invite a volunteer to read aloud, the first commandment, Exodus 20:2-3.

- Though we don't typically worship gods in the way the ancient Israelites did, when we broaden the definition of "other gods" to include those things or people we put our trust in, or define ourselves by, or put in a place of authority in our lives, it's easy to see there are many gods we can easily put before the Lord. What are some "gods" you see people worshipping today? (*wealth, status, fame, comfort, tradition, family, careers, and so forth—point out how even good things can become idols*)

Near the end of the first chapter, Hamilton writes:

> *When I began my study of the Ten Commandments, I could think of five or six of the commandments I wrestled with in one way or another, but the first commandment didn't come*

to mind. The more I reflected on what constitutes a false god, however, the more I realized that this might be the commandment I am most tempted to break.

- After reading through this chapter, how do you identify with the author in this way?

As we move through this study, we will see how Jesus's words speak to each of the commandments, and how he turns every "thou shalt not" into a positive "do this instead."

- Read aloud, or invite a volunteer to read aloud, Jesus's words in Matthew 22:37-38. How does this command speak to every area of our lives?

Wrapping Up

The first commandment forces us to consider the question, "What is at the center of your life?"

- Take a few minutes to quietly reflect on what the Lord has to say to you about that question, and what the true answer might be. How is God asking you to respond to God today?

Closing Prayer

Holy and loving God, you know our hearts so well, and that we are so easily distracted in our devotion to you. Thank you for loving us and choosing us to be your children. Help us to recognize the false gods in our lives and to constantly turn our hearts back to you. Thank you for your faithfulness to us; in Jesus's name. Amen.

TWO

THE IDOLS WE KEEP

Planning the Session

Session Goals

Through conversation, activities, and reflection, participants will:

- reflect on what the second commandment has to say about the modern-day idols we tend to worship;
- explore how God taught the Israelites a new way to worship God; and
- consider what it means to reflect God's image in our own lives.

Biblical Foundation

Exodus 20:4-5; Exodus 32:1-5; Matthew 6:24; Colossians 1:15, 19

Before the Session

- Set up a table in the room with nametags, markers, Bibles, extra copies of *Words of Life*, paper, and pencils or pens.
- Prepare your DVD player or computer to play this week's video segment.
- If possible, have a whiteboard or chart paper and markers or a chalkboard and chalk available for use during the session. Write this session's commandment so that it is visible for all participants:

Do not make an idol for yourself—no form whatsoever—of anything in the sky above or on the earth below or in the waters under the earth. Do not bow down to them or worship them.

(Exodus 20:4-5)

17

Getting Started

Opening Activity

Greet participants as they arrive. Invite them to make a nametag and, if available, pick up either a Bible or a copy of *Words of Life,* or both if they did not bring them.

Say: "Today we will explore how, in the second commandment, God challenged God's people to embrace new ways of worshipping God and experiencing God's presence."

Ask:

- When do you most feel God's presence? Is it in a physical place? through an act or ritual?
- How do these physical experiences help you to better "see" or "feel" God?

Opening Prayer

Holy God, thank you for this time together in which we seek to understand and know you more. As we study today, help us to recognize the idols in our lives and to confront our devotion to them over our relationship with you; in the name of your Son, Jesus Christ, we pray. Amen.

Learning Together

Video Viewing and Discussion

Play the DVD session (each is approximately 10 minutes long), then invite the group to discuss:

- What are your thoughts on seeing the images of the temple of Luxor? How do you think the presence of these temples might have affected the ancient Israelites' perception on how to worship a god?
- How did the Lord use the imagery and statues of the gods of the ancient Egyptians in order to flip the Israelites' understanding of who the Lord was?

Study and Discussion

- Read, or invite a volunteer to read aloud, the second commandment, Exodus 20:4-5.
- At the beginning of the second chapter in his book, Adam Hamilton reminds us:

> *The Jewish tradition, along with Catholics and Lutherans, considers the commandment above to be part of the first commandment. Most other Christians view it as the second. There clearly is a sense in which this commandment forbids devotion and prayer to gods other than Yahweh. But those who consider it its own commandment believe it is not merely prohibiting the worship of images and idols of false gods but also prohibiting the making, praying to, and worshipping of idols that were intended to represent Yahweh himself.*

God did not want Israel to follow the other cultures' habits of making images or idols (like Egypt did) of God. God wanted to teach the Israelites a different way to worship God.

- Read aloud, or invite a volunteer to read aloud, Exodus 32:1-5. What do you imagine the Israelites were feeling as they waited for Moses to return with instructions from God?
- Why do you think they asked Aaron to make them an idol? (*They wanted an idol of their God, Yahweh, in the same way that the Egyptians had idols of their gods. That is what they had been used to.*)

Hamilton writes,

> *Two things are clear in this episode: First, humans prefer to worship gods they can see—for most of us, seeing is believing. And second, God rejected idols or images made to represent him;*

19

nothing created either by God or by humans can adequately express the glory of God. For God, believing is seeing.

- Have you ever felt that you needed to see something in order to believe it? Do you ever feel that way when it comes to God?
- Like the ancient Israelites, we struggle with worshipping false gods in the form of material objects. How have you seen this to be true in your own life, or in the lives of others?
- Jesus speaks frequently of one of these idols—wealth—for example, in Matthew 6:24. Read that verse aloud. In what ways does our culture worship wealth?
- How does Jesus say wealth affects Christians specifically?

In the section "The Image of the Invisible God," the author writes,

The second commandment prohibits us, as humans, from making idols or forms that represent God, or things that take the place of God. Yet the Bible tells us of two ways in which God has made his image visible.

- Read aloud, or invite a volunteer to read aloud, Colossians 1:15 and 19. In whom did God make God's image visible? (*Jesus himself is God in the flesh, given to us that we might see, we might know, and we might believe.*)
- How does reflecting on who Jesus was and what he did for us help you to "see" or experience God more clearly?
- The second image is us! God created us in God's image (see Genesis 1:27), and "when we walk with

Christ," Hamilton writes, "when we seek to do his will, when we love God with our whole heart and we love our neighbor as we love ourselves, we actually reflect the image of God." When has someone been a reflection of God to you?

Wrapping Up

The second commandment challenges us to think about what it means to reflect the image of God. Take a few minutes to pray and consider:

- How might you be the reflection of God to someone this week?

Closing Prayer

Father, we are humbled to be created in your image. Help us to put our hope in you above all else in our lives, worshipping you alone. Thank you for the faith to know that you are always with us and always for us; in Jesus's name. Amen.

THREE

"I SWEAR TO GOD!"

Planning the Session

Session Goals

Through conversation, activities, and reflection, participants will:

- consider what the third commandment has to say about our words and our actions; and
- reflect on what it means to be a disciple of Christ in those words and actions.

Biblical Foundation

Exodus 20:7; Numbers 30:2; Matthew 5:14-16;
Matthew 5:33-37

Before the Session

- Set up a table in the room with nametags, markers, Bibles, extra copies of *Words of Life*, paper, and pencils or pens.
- Prepare your DVD player or computer to play this week's video segment.
- If possible, have a whiteboard or chart paper and markers or a chalkboard and chalk available for use during the session. Write this session's commandment so that it is visible for all participants:

  Do not use the LORD your God's name as if it were of no significance; the LORD won't forgive anyone who uses his name that way.
  (Exodus 20:7)

22

Getting Started

Opening Activity

Greet participants as they arrive. Invite them to make a nametag and, if available, pick up either a Bible or a copy of *Words of Life*, or both if they did not bring them.

Say: "Last week we discussed what it means to reflect God's image in the world around us."

Encourage participants to share:

- What is one instance in which you saw God reflected in someone this week?

Say: "Today we will explore the third commandment, which asks us to consider if our words and actions match up to our identities as disciples of Christ."

Opening Prayer

Heavenly Father, meet us today as we dive deeper into your commandments and learn more about the truths your Word has for us. Open our hearts that we might draw closer to you today; in Jesus's name. Amen.

Learning Together

Video Viewing and Discussion

Play the DVD session (each is approximately 10 minutes long), then invite the group to discuss:

- What struck you most about Adam Hamilton and Rabbi Nemitoff's discussion about what it means to violate the third commandment?
- Hamilton points out that the question this commandment poses to us is, "Am I a good representation of the name of God? Am I bearing God's name well?" When have you seen or experienced someone representing God well?

Study and Discussion

- Read aloud, or invite a volunteer to read aloud, the third commandment, Exodus 20:7.

This commandment invites us to consider that how we use God's name is a reflection of our reverence and respect (or lack thereof) toward God. (Maybe you've more commonly heard this as "do not take the Lord's name in vain.") Hamilton tells us that profanity is not the primary thing Moses or God had in mind with the third commandment. In the section "Promise Keeping and Truth Telling," Hamilton writes,

> *Many scholars have suggested that the primary intent of this commandment had to do with the practice of swearing oaths in the name of God. It called the ancient Israelites (and us) to keep their promises and tell the truth.*
>
> *In the ancient world, when people made promises or were seeking to emphasize that they were telling the truth, they would swear by the name of their god.*

- What are some modern-day oaths or vows that we make? (*wedding vows, "handshake" deals, written contracts, verbal promises, and so forth*)
- Read aloud Numbers 30:2. What does this verse say about the importance of the promises we make?

Hamilton continues,

> *Having considered a couple applications of the third commandment, let's turn now to how Jesus interpreted and applied it. Once again, Jesus's teaching moves from the "thou shalt not" of the commandment to a positive ethic for how we're meant to live our lives, an ethic that is ultimately life-giving.*

- Read aloud Matthew 5:33-37. What is Jesus commanding us to do in these verses? (*Be people of integrity and honesty in our words, do not make false promises, and so forth.*) Why do you think this is important?

As we learned in the last chapter, God created humanity in the divine image, and we are meant to reflect God's image to one another. At the end of the section titled "Jesus, Truth Telling, and Oath Keeping," Hamilton writes,

> *As God's people, we bear the name of God. And we can speak about God not only through our words but through the way we live our lives.*

- In what ways have you seen people misusing God's name with their words? with their actions?
- When this happens, what effect does it have on those both outside of and inside the church?

In the next section, the author says,

> *The Israelites were God's chosen people, called to be a "light for the nations." They were meant to represent and reveal God's character and will. Later Jesus said the same of his disciples, the church.*

- Read aloud Matthew 5:14-16. How does Jesus describe what it looks like to be his disciple? What does he say about a believer's words and actions?

Just before the final section of this chapter, the author writes,

> *Jesus's approach to keeping this commandment [was] not merely by avoiding profaning God's name but by positively hallowing God's name in our words and in our deeds.*

25

- In what ways do you struggle to reflect God's love in your daily life?

Wrapping Up

In the final section of the third chapter, the author points out,

> In Matthew, Jesus says, "Let your light shine before people, so they can see the good things you do and praise your Father who is in heaven" (Matthew 5:16). To a similar end, it's often been said that you are the only sermon some people will hear, the only Bible some will read, and the only image of God some will ever see.

We will never be perfect, but we can strive to be truth tellers and promise keepers, honoring God's name in our thoughts, words, and deeds. As we wrap up this week, consider the following:

- Through this chapter's study, have you realized any ways in which you've misrepresented God in your words or actions? Is God calling you to make amends to someone in this area of your life?
- As a disciple of Christ, in what areas is the Lord calling you to grow in love in your words and in your interactions with others?

Closing Prayer

Lord, we praise and revere your name. Help us to honor you in all we say and all we do, realizing that we are your hands and feet in this world. In our words, thoughts, and deeds, help us to bring glory to your name; in Jesus's name. Amen.

FOUR

REDISCOVERING THE JOY OF SABBATH

Planning the Session

Session Goals

Through conversation, activities, and reflection, participants will:

- learn about God's intentions for the Sabbath;
- consider what it means to "remember" the Sabbath and to keep it holy; and
- reflect on Jesus's interpretation of the Sabbath and consider how to reclaim it in their lives.

Biblical Foundation

Exodus 20:8-11; Deuteronomy 5:15; Matthew 12:9-14; Mark 2:27

Before the Session

- Set up a table in the room with nametags, markers, Bibles, extra copies of *Words of Life*, paper, and pencils or pens.
- Prepare your DVD player or computer to play this week's video segment.
- If possible, have a whiteboard or chart paper and markers or a chalkboard and chalk available for use during the session. Write this session's commandment so that it is visible for all participants:

Remember the Sabbath day and treat it as holy.
(Exodus 20:8)

27

Getting Started

Opening Activity

Greet participants as they arrive. Invite them to make a nametag and, if available, pick up either a Bible or a copy of *Words of Life,* or both if they did not bring them.

Begin your time by encouraging participants to share and discuss:

- Describe your ideal day "off." What would it look like? Who would you spend it with? What would you do—or *not* do?

This week we will explore the fourth commandment, in which God creates and gives instructions for the Sabbath, and how God's followers should observe it.

Opening Prayer

Lord, thank you for another opportunity to gather and learn more about your desire for our lives—how we live, how we rest, how we worship, and how we can best honor you. We thank you for your presence among us today; in Jesus's name. Amen.

Learning Together

Video Viewing and Discussion

Play the DVD session (each is approximately 10 minutes long), then invite the group to discuss:

- Throughout the ages, the image of water is often described as a source of life and relaxation. What do you feel as you see these images of the Nile River? What are some physical places that renew you?
- Rabbi Nemitoff describes how the Sabbath is central to the life of the Jewish people. In what ways does the description of the Jewish Sabbath (or Shabbat) appeal to you?

Study and Discussion

- Read aloud, or invite someone to read aloud, the fourth commandment, Exodus 20:8-11.

In the section titled "God's Concern for Workers," Adam Hamilton writes,

> *We live in a time when having at least one day off per week is assumed, and for many people, two days off is the norm. But when we look at the ancient world, there is no evidence that any nation or peoples observed a required day of rest until the advent of the Ten Commandments. Work was limited by the number of hours of daylight and was expected to take place every day....*
>
> *The story of God's liberation of the Israelites from Egypt begins with God's concern for the harsh working conditions they labored in. The insistence that the Israelites keep the Sabbath, and that they grant a Sabbath to their laborers and even their animals, was again a reflection of God's concern about quality of life, particularly for those who otherwise would not have a day of rest.*

- Consider the working conditions of the Israelites. How do you imagine they reacted to this command?
- How important has the Sabbath been in your life? Is it something you regularly practice, or does it often get overrun by other things?

At the end of that section, Hamilton writes,

> *The Sabbath is the gift of a loving God who cares for his people, who wishes for them a good and beautiful life.*

29

- How does knowing God's intention for the Sabbath change your perspective on it?

Hamilton writes at the end of the next section,

> *The Sabbath is not just about resting. It is about remembering, reflecting, celebrating God's work in creating the world with all of its blessings, and pondering God's deliverance and our identity as his people.*

- Read aloud Deuteronomy 5:15. In what ways do you take time to remember what God has done for you?
- The command goes on to tell us that we are to treat the Sabbath as holy, or set apart for God. What are some practical ways to "set apart" a day for God?

Exodus 31:13 says, "Be sure to keep my sabbaths, because the Sabbath is a sign between me and you in every generation so you will know that I am the LORD who makes you holy." Hamilton puts this into context in the section "Counting the Cost," writing,

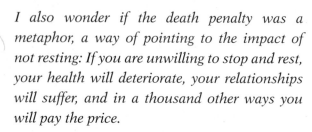

> *I also wonder if the death penalty was a metaphor, a way of pointing to the impact of not resting: If you are unwilling to stop and rest, your health will deteriorate, your relationships will suffer, and in a thousand other ways you will pay the price.*

- How does this perspective resonate with you?

In the following section, Hamilton writes:

> *So the Sabbath is a gift, and it is a rule to live by. But the challenge of rules, even good ones, is that we can get so focused on the rule that we end up missing its intent.*

30

Say: "The debate about what does and does not constitute work on the Sabbath was one of the areas in which Jesus challenged people to look beyond the rule to better understand the heart of God."

- Read aloud Matthew 12:9-14, and then Mark 2:27.

Hamilton adds these words:

> *Notice, however, that Jesus doesn't say, "The Sabbath is not important" or "You don't have to observe the Sabbath." Jesus removes the nitpicking over definitions, but he never sets aside the Sabbath itself. The Sabbath is clearly important to Jesus. He routinely enters the synagogue on the Sabbath. He ministers and teaches on the Sabbath. He helps others on the Sabbath. And presumably, he rests and renews with his disciples on the Sabbath. Jesus moves from a Sabbath observance built around rules to one built around people. This included rest and renewal, and for Jesus, it seems also to have included gathering for prayer in the synagogue. He saw that the intent of the Sabbath was to bless God's people, and he spent his Sabbaths doing just that.*

- Who does Jesus say the Sabbath was created for?
- In what ways does Jesus's view on the Sabbath challenge, or confirm, the way you have approached the Sabbath in your own life?

Wrapping Up

Near the end of the chapter, the author writes,

> *My hunch is that some of you reading this book are, like me, overcommitted people who have a*

31

hard time saying no. And often it is your health, your family, and your faith that suffer for it. I think God wants to say to those who struggle with this, "Remember the Sabbath and keep it holy." We should work hard during the week and give our best. But one day in seven, we're meant to get off the hamster wheel.

- How do you identify with what the author says about our inability to say no?
- In what ways can you reclaim the Sabbath in your own life?
- Hamilton asked you to identify four things that renew you—that bring you joy—that you haven't done in a while, or haven't done enough of lately. If you haven't done so already, take a few moments to write those things down. (**Note to Leader:** If you have time, you might ask participants to share their responses with one another.)

Closing Prayer

Lord God, thank you for the gift of the Sabbath. Help us to see that your care for us extends to all areas of our lives, and that when we follow your plan, it's always for our best; in Jesus's name. Amen.

FIVE

A QUESTION OF HONOR

Planning the Session

Session Goals

Through conversation, activities, and reflection, participants will:

- learn about what it means to "honor" one's parents and elders;
- reflect on how Jesus shows us how to live out this commandment; and
- consider how the Lord is leading them to consider the ramifications of this commandment in their own parent/child relationships.

Biblical Foundation

Exodus 20:12; John 2:1-11; John 19:25-27; Romans 13:8

Before the Session

- Set up a table in the room with nametags, markers, Bibles, extra copies of *Words of Life*, paper, and pencils or pens.
- Prepare your DVD player or computer to play this week's video segment.
- If possible, have a whiteboard or chart paper and markers or a chalkboard and chalk available for use during the session. Write this session's commandment so that it is visible for all participants:

*Honor your father and your mother so that
your life will be long on the fertile land that the
Lord your God is giving you.*

(Exodus 20:12)

Getting Started

Opening Activity

Greet participants as they arrive. Invite them to make a nametag and, if available, pick up either a Bible or a copy of *Words of Life*, or both if they did not bring them.

Say: "Today we will look at the fifth commandment, which teaches us about honoring our parents and our elders."

Ask:

- Who is an elder (a parent, grandparent, teacher, neighbor, relative, friend) who has made an impact on your life in some way? What has he or she taught you?

Opening Prayer

Eternal God, we give you thanks for the gift of time and age, and those in our lives who have passed down so much wisdom and love to us. Help us today to better understand this command to honor our parents and our elders, Lord. Thank you for your presence today; in Jesus's name. Amen.

Learning Together

Video Viewing and Discussion

Play the DVD session (each is approximately 10 minutes long), then invite the group to discuss:

- In this video, Adam Hamilton shows us the Egyptian Book of the Dead and describes what the Egyptians believed about judgment and the afterlife. How does what they believe contrast with what our Christian faith teaches?

- How is the footage of ancient Egypt shaping your view of the Ten Commandments and your imagination about the world of the ancient Israelites?
- Rabbi Nemitoff points out the "positive" obligation he feels toward his mother, and how it affects his care for her. How does his view change your perspective on what it means to care for parents or other relatives?

Study and Discussion

As we've already discussed, traditional teaching holds that the first tablet that Moses brought down from Mount Sinai contained the first four commandments, which were focused on living in right relationship with God. The second tablet contained the six commandments focused on living in right relationship with one's fellow human beings. With the fifth commandment, we begin our study of the second tablet.

- Read aloud Exodus 20:12. What has been your experience with this commandment to "honor your father and your mother"?

  Note to Leader: Be aware that you may have some participants who are triggered or uncomfortable with this commandment because they have experienced abuse or neglect at the hands of a parent. Be sure and point out that abuse is never okay and that this commandment is not intended to protect or affirm an abusive parent's behavior. Hamilton discusses this at some length at the beginning of the fifth chapter in his book. If you feel that your group could benefit from discussing those points, please take the time to do so.

- In all likelihood, you learned about or heard this commandment when you were a child, and it was probably linked to a directive that you just needed to obey your parents. But as adults, this directive becomes less about obedience to our parents and more about giving them "weight." How does Hamilton describe what it means to give our parents/elders "weight"? (*taking them seriously, considering their needs*)
- As an adult, how do you understand your role as your parents' child? What does that look like, practically, for you?
- What have you discovered about the "love languages" of the elders in your life? How has that knowledge changed your relationship with them?

In the section "The Primary Meaning of Honor? Caring for the Aging," Hamilton points out, "Many scholars believe that the fifth commandment's primary intent was to ensure people cared for the elderly." Jesus quotes this commandment twice in the Gospels, and then powerfully illustrates the heart behind the commandment in two instances.

- Read aloud John 2:1-11. How did Jesus honor his mother in this story? (*because his mother asked, he performs his first miracle, transforming water into wine*)
- In John 19:25-27, while he was on the cross, what does Jesus ask of John ("the disciple whom he loved")? What does this tell us about Jesus? (*that he was caring for and providing for his mother and her physical care, even in his death*)
- Hamilton also discusses taking care of older adults to whom we are not related. What is Jesus saying to us about caring for those elderly who may not be our family? What obligation do we have to those individuals?

Wrapping Up

In Romans 13:8, Paul states a powerful truth: "Don't be in debt to anyone, except for the obligation to love each other. Whoever loves another person has fulfilled the Law." We should keep this in mind as we seek to honor, love, and care for others, especially those who are aging. The heart of the fifth commandment is not about obligation, but about love.

- Does Romans 13:8 change your perspective on the fifth commandment?
- By honoring our parents and older adults, we model for our children, and the generations that follow, how they should honor us when we reach "old age" ourselves. In what ways have you seen this to be true?
- When thinking of our own children, we should consider how to bless them, to encourage them, and to make it as easy as possible for them to honor us in our later years. When and how have you seen other parents do this well for their children? What effect did it have on the parent/child relationship?

Closing Prayer

Jesus, help us as we seek to follow you in honoring others above ourselves. Thank you for loving us enough to sacrifice everything for us. May we honor you as we honor those in our lives who need our care and attention; in Jesus's name. Amen.

SIX

THE TRAGEDY OF VIOLENCE, THE BEAUTY OF MERCY

Planning the Session

Session Goals

Through conversation, activities, and reflection, participants will:

- learn about God's heart and desire for God's creation to live in peace with one another; and
- reflect on how Jesus shows us how to live out the sixth commandment.

Biblical Foundation

Genesis 9:5-6; Exodus 20:13; Isaiah 2:4; Isaiah 11:6-7, 9a; Matthew 5:21-22; Matthew 5:43-45; Ephesians 4:29

Before the Session

- Set up a table in the room with nametags, markers, Bibles, extra copies of *Words of Life*, paper, and pencils or pens.
- Prepare your DVD player or computer to play this week's video segment.
- If possible, have a whiteboard or chart paper and markers or a chalkboard and chalk available for use during the session. Write this session's commandment so that it is visible for all participants:

Do not kill.
  (Exodus 20:13)

Getting Started

Opening Activity

Greet participants as they arrive. Invite them to make a nametag and, if available, pick up either a Bible or a copy of *Words of Life*, or both if they did not bring them.

Say: "Today we will look at the sixth commandment, which is short, but as we'll discover, is loaded with meaning. It is, 'Do not kill' (Exodus 20.13)."

Near the beginning of the sixth chapter in his book, Adam Hamilton points out,

> *The prohibition against killing appears in nearly every ancient law code. It has been the most basic of ethical and moral requirements since the beginning of civilization. Yet the last hundred years have been the deadliest in the history of the human race.... It seems clear that humanity has utterly failed to abide by this most basic of ethical imperatives.*

- When was the last time you were confronted with an act of violence (either personally or something you learned about through the media)? What was your reaction or response?

Though our world can sometimes seem dangerous and unpredictable, as we'll study today, God desires peace for us, and Jesus teaches us about what it means to live in a way that honors God's image in each of us.

Opening Prayer

Lord, we praise you for being present here with us today and every day. Help us to know you better through each and every commandment we explore and to learn more about your desire and hope for our lives. We praise you as the God of peace, even in our turbulent world; in Jesus's name. Amen.

Learning Together

Video Viewing and Discussion

Play the DVD session (each is approximately 10 minutes long), then invite the group to discuss:

- In his younger years, Moses killed a man. How do you imagine Moses must have felt when God gave him this commandment for Israel?
- Rabbi Nemitoff suggests that a more accurate translation of this commandment is "do not murder" and that it connects back to the first commandment in the Jewish tradition ("I am God"). What is that connection? (*Murdering someone, who is made in God's image, is like murdering God.*)
- How does Jesus flip this commandment into a "thou shalt"? *Love your enemy*

Study and Discussion

The Bible's first murder happens very early in Scripture, in Genesis 4. Cain kills his brother Abel out of jealousy, resentment, and bitterness. Soon after, the world seems consumed with violence, and God is heartbroken. He sends a flood to cleanse the earth and start anew. Following the flood we read this pronouncement from God: "Whoever sheds human blood, / by a human his blood will be shed; / for in the divine image / God made human beings" (Genesis 9:6). Regarding this verse, Hamilton writes at the end of the section "Murder in the Bible,"

> This provides a theological basis for human rights in Western civilization. Harming a human being is an offense against God. To kill is to destroy God's possession...and to violate someone who was created in God's image.

40

- Read aloud Isaiah 2:4 and Isaiah 11:6-7, 9a. What do these verses say about God's desire for the world? (*that God desires peace, and a world without violence*)

Hamilton writes,

> *This picture of a world without violence is a picture of God's ideal world—perhaps even a picture of heaven. It points to a world where no one, not even the animals, kills. But we don't live in that world yet.*

- In this chapter, Hamilton addresses self-defense, war, and manslaughter in relation to this commandment. What are your thoughts on his conclusions?

Early in this chapter, Hamilton writes,

> *Jesus broadened the meaning of this command. We'll find that his words have implications far beyond the taking of another human life—words that have power to liberate us from bitterness and resentment and replace them with freedom and joy.*

- Read aloud Jesus's words in Matthew 5:21-22 from the Sermon on the Mount. What emotion does Jesus connect with the sixth commandment? (*anger*)
- In Jesus's view, the sixth commandment is not just about killing others, but harming them, insulting them, or hurting them. How have you seen anger destroy a relationship?
- Again in the Sermon on the Mount, Jesus goes even further than just not hurting your enemies. Read aloud Matthew 5:43-45. What does Jesus command instead?

41

In the chapter's final section, the author writes,

> *When we read the commandments through the eyes of Jesus, we recognize that the command prohibiting murder is ultimately a command calling for love. Loving one's enemy does not mean summoning warm feelings for them. It is to see them as a human being created in the image of God, and to treat them as you wish they had treated you.*
>
> *Often this kind of love looks like mercy.*

- In what ways have you seen God be merciful to you?
- When we are hurt, our hearts long for vengeance, but Jesus teaches forgiveness. And remember—he even extended that forgiveness to those people who put him to death (see Luke 23:34). Have you ever been on the giving or receiving end of undeserved mercy from another? What effect did that gift have on everyone involved?

Wrapping Up

The author says that he's asked his congregation to memorize Ephesians 4:29:

> *Don't let any foul words come out of your mouth. Only say what is helpful when it is needed for building up the community so that it benefits those who hear what you say.*

This verse is so important, because as Hamilton writes at the end of the chapter,

> *Moses taught us,* Do not kill. *But Jesus said it goes deeper than that. Don't harm others. Don't*

return insult for insult. Forgive others and love your enemies. In doing so, you will find the good and beautiful life.

- Have you ever felt that this sixth commandment—do not kill—wasn't relevant to you? How has this study changed your view on this commandment's intent?
- In what ways is the Lord asking you to forgive or love others in a way you might not have considered before?

Closing Prayer

Heavenly Father, you know our greatest needs, even when we aren't aware of them. Search our hearts, Lord, and help us to see the ways in which we hurt others with our words and actions. Help us to let go of any bitterness or anger we are harboring and embrace the love you so graciously give us so that we can extend that to others; in Jesus's name. Amen.

SEVEN

FAITHFULNESS IN AN AGE OF PORN

Planning the Session

Session Goals

Through conversation, activities, and reflection, participants will:

- consider the small ways that sin can enter our lives and discover how to stop something before it starts; and
- learn what Jesus reveals about our hearts through this commandment.

Biblical Foundation

Genesis 1:27-28; Genesis 3:16; Exodus 20:14;
Matthew 5:27-28; John 8:1-11; James 1:13-15

Before the Session

- Set up a table in the room with nametags, markers, Bibles, extra copies of *Words of Life*, paper, and pencils or pens.
- Prepare your DVD player or computer to play this week's video segment.
- If possible, have a whiteboard or chart paper and markers or a chalkboard and chalk available for use during the session. Write this session's commandment so that it is visible for all participants:

  Do not commit adultery.
  (Exodus 20:14)

44

Getting Started

Opening Activity

Greet participants as they arrive. Invite them to make a nametag and, if available, pick up either a Bible or a copy of *Words of Life*, or both if they did not bring them.

Say: "Today we will look at the seventh commandment, which continues to teach us about how to live in right relationship with others. These commandments are meant to serve as guardrails and guideposts in our lives, keeping us safe and off of dangerous paths."

Ask:

open

- Has there been a time in your life when you realized that the Lord was speaking to you about a "small" sin that had the potential to get really dangerous? What did God show you about that sin?

Opening Prayer

Father, thank you for the gift of your Word, which serves as a constant light along the path of our lives. Continue to teach us today about your desire for our thoughts and actions, especially in how we live in relation to others; in Jesus's name. Amen.

Learning Together

Video Viewing and Discussion

Play the DVD session (each is approximately 10 minutes long), then invite the group to discuss:

- As you learn about the life of Hatshepsut, who was one of the few female pharaohs of Egypt, what do you learn about the value of women in the ancient world?
- How does Rabbi Nemitoff say that this command-ment connects with the second commandment

("have no other gods before me")? (*Our relationship is to be with one God and marriage is a commitment to one person.*)

- Jesus points out that this commandment is not just about what we do but what we think. What are some ways that we can train our minds to be holy? (*studying scripture, praying, having accountability, and so forth*)

Study and Discussion'

As we have discussed, the first four commandments that God gave Moses were instructions about how we live in relation to God, and the last six are related to how we live with one another. Today we will look at the seventh commandment, "Do not commit adultery" (Exodus 20:14). This commandment follows just after the prohibition against murder, which points to the severity of this transgression against one's neighbor.

- Adultery was evidently a prevalent issue in the ancient world, as most cultures had rules against it. How does Adam Hamilton describe adultery in these highly patriarchal societies? Who did the rule against adultery typically protect? (Adultery was, technically, a violation of a husband's rights that took place when another man slept with his wife. But men could have several wives, so this was really just to protect a man's "property.")
- Read aloud Genesis 1:27-28. What was God's design for the relationship between husband and wife? (*that they would be partners*)
- When Adam and Eve were cast out of Eden, what did sin do to their relationship? (See Genesis 3:16.) (*created a hierarchy—a patriarchy*)

Hamilton writes in the first section of the chapter,

I believe that patriarchy and the subordination of women in human society were never God's will. Genesis 3:16 was not prescriptive. Rather, the verse was descriptive—it was announcing how things would be in a broken world outside of Eden. It is how relationships would be distorted by sin and the difference in physical strength generally seen between the genders. This patriarchy was seen as normative across the ancient world. But it was not God's original or intended will.

- Have you considered this interpretation before? What are your thoughts on this?

Thinking about the patriarchal society of the ancient Israelites leads us to the story of King David and Bathsheba. Hamilton breaks down their story into what he describes as the "anatomy of an affair." David sees Bathsheba bathing and doesn't look away. Instead, he allows a "maybe" to enter his mind and grow into a dangerous desire.

- Read aloud James 1:13-15. What does this passage say about the dangers of our desires? How does this relate directly to David's actions?
- How can allowing a "maybe"—the possibility of a sin—open the door to further sin?
- Read aloud Matthew 5:27-28. How does Jesus say we should handle even the slightest bit of temptation? (*Here Jesus uses prophetic hyperbole as a way of saying how serious sin can get. It's a warning to be on constant guard with our thoughts in particular.*)

Near the end of the chapter, the author writes,

Jesus set impossible standards in his teachings and ministry. He forbade us from even looking

47

at another with lust in our hearts. Yet when a woman was caught in the very act of adultery, Jesus refused to condemn her....Jesus forgave her and forced her accusers to set her free.

- Read aloud John 8:1-11. How do you imagine Jesus's words sounded to this woman? What do you imagine about her reaction?
- Even here, on one of the "top-ten" sins, Jesus shows mercy. What does that tell us about his mercy toward us when we sin?

Wrapping Up

What was true for this woman is also true for us. Though the Lord offers us infinite forgiveness through Jesus, our sin can also lead to serious and devastating consequences. Thankfully we have our Lord's words to serve as guardrails and guideposts as we live our lives.

- In this chapter, Hamilton gives us Five Rs of Resisting Temptation. Do any of these resonate with you? Take a few minutes to read through these five points, and ask the Lord to open your eyes to any "maybes" that might be leading you down a dangerous path.

Closing Prayer

Lord, thank you for your Word, which provides us with guardrails and guideposts that help us avoid the pain and destruction that sin wreaks upon our world. Thank you for the forgiveness you so graciously extend when we do mess up. Your faithfulness to us is beautiful and your grace absolute. We praise you for that; in Jesus's name. Amen.

EIGHT

WE'RE ALL THIEVES.
YES, EVEN YOU.

Planning the Session

Session Goals

Through conversation, activities, and reflection, participants will:

- learn about how the eighth commandment applies to
  us in ways we might not have realized;
- consider the everyday implications of this commandment; and
- reflect on how Jesus shows us how to live out of a
  sense of generosity.

Biblical Foundation

Exodus 20:15; Proverbs 22:9; Matthew 7:12;
Matthew 25:34-36; Luke 12:48b; James 5:1-5

Before the Session

- Set up a table in the room with nametags, markers,
  Bibles, extra copies of *Words of Life*, paper, and
  pencils or pens.
- Prepare your DVD player or computer to play this
  week's video segment.
- If possible, have a whiteboard or chart paper and
  markers or a chalkboard and chalk available for use
  during the session. Write this session's commandment so that it is visible for all participants:

  Do not steal.
  (Exodus 20:15)

Getting Started

Opening Activity

Greet participants as they arrive. Invite them to make a nametag and, if available, pick up either a Bible or a copy of *Words of Life*, or both if they did not bring them.

Say: "Today we will explore the eighth commandment and the heart behind what it means. It was not meant to just stop us from stealing, but to learn to live in generosity and contentment."

Ask:

- In what areas of your life do you struggle with feeling as though you don't have enough? How do you think that affects your motivations and behavior? (*This could be anything, from time to money to food to certain possessions, and so forth.*)

Opening Prayer

Lord, speak to us today through the words of this commandment. As we explore what it means to steal, and what it means to live in generosity, help us to examine our hearts for the ways in which our own greed or sense of scarcity affects the way we treat others; in Jesus's name. Amen.

Learning Together

Video Viewing and Discussion

Play the DVD session (each is approximately 10 minutes long), then invite the group to discuss:

- Adam Hamilton and Art Nemitoff suggest that this commandment is not as straightforward as it seems on the surface. After viewing their conversation, what stands out to you as ways that you have violated this commandment, or been tempted to?

- What do you think of the connection between this commandment and the third commandment, about taking the Lord's name in vain? How is stealing akin to claiming a godlike status for yourself?
- Hamilton suggests that not giving our offerings to God is a form of stealing, in the sense of withholding what rightfully belongs to God. How does this change or challenge your understanding of giving to the church or to charitable organizations?

Study and Discussion

The eighth commandment is "Do not steal" (Exodus 20:15). We can assume that this one made it onto the "top-ten" list because it was deemed serious and it was a problem in the early Israelite community.

This commandment seems pretty straightforward—don't take other people's things, right? For most of us, that probably seems like an easy commandment to keep; but let's take it a step further and consider Jesus's words that we have come to know as the "Golden Rule."

- Read aloud Matthew 7:12. How does this relate to the idea of "Finders, Keepers" that we're all familiar with?
- How does this command speak to those of us who would never consider outright stealing or taking what is not ours? Hamilton says he wants to "step on our toes" a bit and explore that question. Were you convicted by any of the common "thefts" he mentioned? Did any other offenses come to mind as you considered his interpretation of stealing?
- How do you respond to Hamilton's thoughts on tithing? Or the suggestion that being late is stealing someone else's time?
- Read aloud James 5:1-5. How do these verses speak to today's marketplace, and to those of us who employ others?

51

Here's the point: we're all thieves. Hamilton states,

> *We've all violated the eighth commandment,*
> *and God is calling us to stop stealing.*

Jesus cites this eighth commandment as one of those essential to practice in order to inherit eternal life (see Matthew 19:18; Mark 10:19; and Luke 18:20); but, as we've seen throughout, Jesus replaces the prohibitive "thou shalt not" with a positive "thou shalt."

In the section titled "Jesus and the Eighth Commandment," Hamilton writes,

> *If stealing is about taking what isn't yours (time, money, property, even things like accolades), its antidote would be giving what you have to those who have no right to expect it.*

- Read aloud Proverbs 22:9. How does this scripture describe generous people? (*happy, because they give*)
- One of Jesus's most powerful parables is found in Matthew 25:34-36. Read it aloud, or invite a volunteer to read it aloud. Here Jesus describes the blessing of the righteous on the final judgment day. How do these words instruct us to live? (*to care for others' needs and to welcome the stranger and those in desperation*)
- Jesus makes it clear that generosity, not greed or desire, is meant to be our way of life. What are some ways this chapter points out how we can exercise generosity? Do any of these resonate with you?

Note to Leader: If you'd like to keep exploring, here are some other verses to consider on generosity and greed: Matthew 5:42; Matthew 6:19-21; Matthew 6:24; Luke 6:38; Luke 12:15; Proverbs 11:25.

Wrapping Up

Two thieves were crucified with Jesus, one on either side. One recognized who Jesus was, and in his final moments, Jesus extended grace and mercy to him. In the last section, Hamilton writes,

> *I can't end without mentioning the one Gospel story in which Jesus himself interacted with two convicted thieves....I didn't realize how much of [a thief] I was until I really studied the eighth commandment. But I love the fact that, to the end, Jesus was still forgiving sinners. And the final sinner Jesus forgave before he died was a thief.*

- In what ways has this chapter opened your eyes to the heart behind the eighth commandment (Do not steal)?
- Read aloud Luke 12:48b. In this verse, Jesus captured both the call to generosity and the sense of responsibility we're meant to have as those who follow him. In what area of your life have you been given much, and how do you sense God calling you to give out of that abundance?

Closing Prayer

Father God, you have blessed us abundantly in so many ways. Help us to fight the greed that so easily entangles us and to realize that you have blessed us so that we can pass that blessing along to others in your name. Thank you for your extravagant grace when we fail in this; in Jesus's name. Amen.

NINE

STICKS, STONES, AND THE POWER OF WORDS

Planning the Session

Session Goals

Through conversation, activities, and reflection, participants will:

- learn about how the ninth commandment applies to our everyday lives;
- consider the weight of our words and the power of our speech; and
- reflect on how Jesus modeled humility and grace toward those who slandered him.

Biblical Foundation

Exodus 20:16; James 1:26; James 3:6-10; Ephesians 4:29; Philippians 2:3-5

Before the Session

- Set up a table in the room with nametags, markers, Bibles, extra copies of *Words of Life*, paper, and pencils or pens.
- Prepare your DVD player or computer to play this week's video segment.
- If possible, have a whiteboard or chart paper and markers or a chalkboard and chalk available for use during the session. Write this session's commandment so that it is visible for all participants:

Do not testify falsely against your neighbor.
(Exodus 20:16)

54

Getting Started

Opening Activity

Greet participants as they arrive. Invite them to make a nametag and, if available, pick up either a Bible or a copy of *Words of Life*, or both if they did not bring them.

Say: "Today we will study the ninth commandment—'Do not testify falsely against your neighbor' (Exodus 20:16)."

Ask:

• What was your reaction to hearing about Darryl Burton's story of false imprisonment?

Opening Prayer

God, thank you for this time in your Word together. As we study how our words affect other people, help us to keep in mind that we are all your children, and each of us deserves respect and consideration because you say we are worthy; in Jesus's name. Amen.

Learning Together

Video Viewing and Discussion

Play the DVD session (each is approximately 10 minutes long), then invite the group to discuss:

• Rabbi Art Nemitoff said that in his tradition, damaging someone's reputation by testifying falsely about them is as serious as murder. Why do you think this is the case?
• When have you witnessed harmful rumors that did irreparable damage? What did it take to make things right, knowing that the rumors could not be undone?
• Why is it so tempting, and arguably easier, to spread false rumors in the age of the internet? What is

the best way for Christians to guard against false testimony online?

Study and Discussion

A system of justice relies on people telling the truth. This was true in the Old Testament system and is true of ours today. When people do not tell the truth, there are consequences for those lies, for all involved.

Adam Hamilton writes,

> *There are always people who are willing to give false testimony if it serves their own interests. False testimony in a courtroom is a crime—we call it perjury. But as we will see, the commandment not to bear false witness against others has application far beyond the courtroom. Ultimately, it is an antidote to the many ways our words can bring others pain.*

- We live in a time when it is increasingly difficult to discern what is true. When it comes to politics, or matters of other news, in what ways do you find it difficult, or muddled, to discern the truth in these situations?
- Social media has made the issue of giving false witness particularly applicable—we can do a lot of harm to someone with just a few keystrokes. How have you seen this to be true?

When it comes to sharing or spreading something on social media, Hamilton says,

> *When we publicly share something as fact that we have not verified as factual, I would suggest we are, perhaps unwittingly, violating the ninth commandment.*

- What do you think about this statement? How diligent are you about fact-checking things on social media?

Jesus modeled for us how we're to respond to others—to see them with love and compassion and resist assuming the worst of them. In most cases, it's our own tongues that he says we need to be most concerned about.

- Read aloud James 3:6-10 and James 1:26. What do these verses say about the power of our speech?

The author points out that the essence of this commandment is "Do not lie." This applies to outright deception, truth stretching, and even hypocrisy. He says that even

> *when our actions are done to impress others, rather than as an attempt to be the person God calls us to be, our actions may be a form of false testimony.*

- How does this interpretation change your view of this command?
- Jesus warned us that the devil is the father of lies (see John 8:44), and that includes the lies that we hear and believe about ourselves. When those lies come, what are some ways we can resist and fight? *(reject the devil in the name of Jesus Christ, who testified with his life that we have value and worth)*
- Sometimes we stretch the truth about others in negative ways to make ourselves look better in comparison. Read aloud Philippians 2:3-5. What does Jesus say is the opposite of this kind of action? *(humility)*
- How did Jesus model humility?

Wrapping Up

In the section "Politics and the Ninth Commandment," Hamilton writes,

> *Every other year there is a major election at the national level. Which means that as you read this chapter, we've either just completed an election or are preparing for one. I want to encourage you to remember this commandment and consciously decide not to share false testimony. People of faith should debate issues, ideas, and approaches to public policy. But let's not pass on as fact what is hearsay. Let's not be purveyors of fake news. Let's love our neighbor, including those on the other side of the political aisle, as we love ourselves.*

- Read aloud Ephesians 4:29, which we've already looked at with regards to the sixth commandment. How does this verse instruct us to interact with others, even when we disagree with them?
- In what ways has this chapter opened your eyes to application of the ninth commandment?

Closing Prayer

Heavenly Father, give us grace in our thoughts and in our speech. Help us to recognize the damage that can be done when we try to find our worth outside of you. Thank you for being ever present and in control of our world and in each of our lives; in Jesus's name. Amen.

TEN

KEEPING UP WITH THE JONESES

Planning the Session

Session Goals

Through conversation, activities, and reflection, participants will:

- consider real-life applications of what it looks like to covet;
- discover how Jesus instructs us to watch out for greed and embrace contentment; and
- reflect on three antidotes to coveting that can help us find contentment.

Biblical Foundation

Exodus 20:17; Proverbs 11:25; Matthew 22:40; Luke 12:15; 1 Timothy 4:6-10; 1 Thessalonians 5:18

Before the Session

- Set up a table in the room with nametags, markers, Bibles, extra copies of *Words of Life*, paper, and pencils or pens.
- Prepare your DVD player or computer to play this week's video segment.
- If possible, have a whiteboard or chart paper and markers or a chalkboard and chalk available for use during the session. Write this session's commandment so that it is visible for all participants:

59

*Do not desire and try to take your neighbor's
house. Do not desire and try to take your
neighbor's wife, male or female servant, ox,
donkey, or anything else that belongs to your
neighbor.*

(Exodus 20:17)

Getting Started

Opening Activity

Greet participants as they arrive. Invite them to make a nametag and, if available, pick up either a Bible or a copy of *Words of Life,* or both if they did not bring them.

Open your group discussion with a question:

- Without thinking about it too much, what is the last thing you wanted to buy for yourself, either because you saw someone else who had it or because you saw an ad that grabbed your interest? (This could be something as small as a new gadget or food item or something as large as a new home.)

Today we will discuss our seemingly constant desire for more, and explore what the Lord has to say to us through the tenth commandment.

Opening Prayer

Lord, speak to us today about our wants and desires through the words of this commandment. Draw us closer to you as we take in your words of life; in Jesus's name. Amen.

Learning Together

Video Viewing and Discussion

Play the DVD session (each is approximately 10 minutes long), then invite the group to discuss:

- Based on what you saw in this video, what would you say is the difference between covetousness and greed?
- What insights did you encounter in the conversation between Adam Hamilton and Rabbi Art Nemitoff that help you understand the danger of coveting in a new way?
- How can we guard against coveting in our lives today?

Study and Discussion

- Read aloud the tenth commandment, Exodus 20:17.

Hamilton writes,

> *This final command speaks profoundly to the human condition. It describes a fundamental struggle we all wrestle with: our desire for what we do not, cannot, or should not have, particularly when that thing belongs to another. The prohibition against coveting, like the other commandments, serves as a guardrail given by God to protect us and a guidepost to help us experience the good and beautiful life God intends.*

The tenth commandment is very much linked to the first commandment—if God is not first in our hearts (commandment one), then it can lead us into searching for our worth in many other places.

- Hamilton points out that, in the Common English Bible translation, "covet" means to "desire and try to take." In light of this, what does the author say was the original sin of Adam and Eve? (*coveting—before they actually ate the fruit, Adam and Eve desired what was not theirs*)

- Read aloud Luke 12:15. The author suggests that for Jesus's audience, greed or covetousness was a very real struggle, as the temptation was ever present to judge their lives—and their worth and identity—based on their possessions. In what ways does this describe our modern-day culture as well?
- Have you ever found yourself believing your identity was wrapped up in your possessions? How did it affect your attitude or actions?
- Read aloud, or invite a volunteer to read aloud, 1 Timothy 4:6-10. What are some ways you have seen the craving for wealth choke out the work of God in someone's life (or your own)?
- In the section "Covetousness in the New Testament," the author gives some modern-day examples of what it might look like to violate this tenth commandment. Are you surprised or convicted by any of his examples?

The book gives three antidotes to coveting that can lead us into contentment. They are gratitude, generosity, and love.

- Read aloud 1 Thessalonians 5:18. What does this verse say God intends for us to do?
- How does gratitude combat coveting? Have you found any practices of gratitude that have changed your desires or wants?
- The author points out a study that says people are happier when they are generous. In what ways have you seen this to be true? Do you struggle with generosity, or giving your things away?
- What does Proverbs 11:25 say generosity does for us? (*refreshes us*)
- Jesus spoke of the two great loves: love for God and love for one's neighbor. He said that "all the Law and the Prophets depend on these two commands" (Matthew 22:40). As we've seen, these two

commands—to love God and to love your neighbor—lie beneath all of the Ten Commandments. Who in your life have you seen live out his or her love of God and of neighbor? In what ways did that person's life affect those around the person?

Wrapping Up

At the end of the chapter, Hamilton writes,

> *In the end, the commandments can shape you and me...powerfully....They were intended to be not onerous burdens but guardrails and guideposts that protect us and point us to the life God intends. My hope in writing this book is that you might find...that these commandments are, in fact, words of life.*

- In what ways has the Lord used this study of the Ten Commandments in your life?
- What guardrails and guideposts do you feel God asking you to establish? Would you like some accountability or encouragement about any specific area the Lord has made you aware of?

Closing Prayer

Jesus, we believe you came to show us the way, the truth, and the life. We are grateful for your love and grace. Help us to live these Ten Commandments, and your words interpreting them. May they shape our lives always; in Jesus's name. Amen.